P9-BZK-176

Blessed Virgin Mary

In Glory

Blessed Virgin Mary

 Poems & Prayers

Stewart, Tabori & Chang
New York

Dedication

To
Zillah Bahar
For Her
Idea
Intelligence
Ingenuity

~

Blessings

Renaissance Masterpieces

VIRGIN AND CHILD
Jean Fouquet

VIRGIN AND CHILD
Carlo Crivelli

VIRGIN ADORING THE CHILD
Fra Filippo Lippi

VIRGIN AND CHILD
Joos van Cleve

MADONNA WITH THE RED APPLE
Hans Memling

MADONNA OF THE TREES
Giovanni Bellini

MADONNA THE MAGNIFICENT
Sandro Botticelli

LITTA MADONNA
Leonardo da Vinci

VIRGIN AND CHILD UNDER THE APPLE TREE
Lucas Cranach the Elder

MADONNA OF BURGOMASTER MEYER
Hans Holbein the Younger

Poems & Prayers

AVE, GENEROSA * YMNUS DE
SANCTA MARIA

TRANSLATED BY CHRISTOPHER PAGE

Abbess Hildegard of Bingen

VIRGIN MOTHER, DAUGHTER OF THY SON

SELECTION

PARADISO * CANTO XXXIII

TRANSLATED BY JOHN CIARDI

Dante Alighieri

NATIVITY OF CHRIST

TRANSLATED BY HENRY WADSWORTH LONGFELLOW

Luis de Góngora

O STAR OF GALILEE

TRANSLATED BY R. R. MADDEN

Girolamo Savonarola

In Glory

In Glory

APPEAL FOR ILLUMINATION
TRANSLATED BY LORD BYRON
Luigi Pulci

ODE TO THE VIRGIN
TRANSLATED BY HELEN LEE PEABODY
Francesco Petrarch

CANTIGA
TRANSLATED BY THOMAS WALSH
Gil Vincente

QUEEN OF THE ANGELS
TRANSLATED BY THOMAS WALSH
Giovanni Boccaccio

STABAT MATER DOLOROSA
TRANSLATED BY RICHARD CRASHAW
Jacopone da Todi

Poems & Prayers

Ave, Generosa

Hail, girl of a noble house,
shimmering
and unpolluted,
you pupil in the eye of chastity,
you essence of sanctity,
which was pleasing to God.

For the Heavenly potion
was poured into you,
in that the Heavenly word
received a raiment of flesh in you.

You are the lily that dazzles,
whom God knew before all others.

{Ymnus de Sancta Maria}

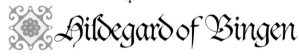

Hildegard of Bingen

TRANSLATED FROM THE LATIN BY CHRISTOPHER PAGE

O most beautiful
and delectable one,
how greatly God delighted in you!
in the clasp of His fire
He implanted in you so that
His son might be suckled by you.

Thus your womb
held joy
when the harmony of all Heaven
chimed out from you,
because, Virgin, you carried Christ
whence your chastity blazed in God.

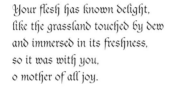

Your flesh has known delight,
like the grassland touched by dew
and immersed in its freshness,
so it was with you,
o mother of all joy.

Now let the sunrise of joy be
over all Ecclesia
and let it resound in music
for the sweetest Virgin,
Mary compelling all praise,
mother of God.
Amen.

·IOANNES·BELLINVS·P·

VIRGIN MOTHER

Virgin Mother, daughter of thy son,
humble beyond all creatures and more exalted,
predestined turning point of God's intention;
thy merit so ennobled human nature
that its divine Creator did not scorn
to make Himself the creature of His own creature.

The Love that was rekindled in Thy womb
sends forth the warmth of the eternal peace
within whose ray this flower has come to bloom.

DAUGHTER OF THY SON

SELECTION
Paradiso
Canto XXXIII

Dante Alighieri

TRANSLATED FROM THE ITALIAN BY JOHN CIARDI

Here, to us, thou art the noon and scope
of Love revealed, and among mortal men,
the living fountain of eternal hope.

Lady, thou art so near God's reckonings
that who seeks grace and does not first seek thee
would have his wish fly upward without wings.

Not only does thy sweet benignity
flow out to all who beg, but oftentimes
thy charity arrives before the plea.

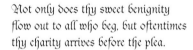

In thee is pity, in thee munificence,
in thee the tenderest heart, in thee unites
all that creation knows of excellence!

Now comes this man who from the final pit
of the universe up to this height has seen,
one by one, the three lives of the spirit.

He prays to thee in fervent supplication
for grace and strength, that he may raise his eyes
to the all-healing final revelation.

And I, who never more desired to see
the vision myself than I do that he may see It,
add my own prayer, and pray that it may be
enough to move you to dispel the trace
of every mortal shadow by thy prayers
and let him see revealed the Sum of Grace.

I pray thee further, all-persuading Queen,
keep whole the natural bent of his affections
and of his powers after his eyes have seen.

The eyes that God reveres and loves the best
glowed on the speaker, making clear the joy
with which true prayer is heard by the most blest.

Those eyes turned then to the Eternal Ray,
through which, we must indeed believe, the eyes
of others do not find such ready way.

And I, who neared the goal of all my nature,
felt my soul, at the climax of its yearning,
suddenly, as it ought, grow calm with rapture.

Little by little as my vision grew
it penetrated further through the aura
of the high lamp which in Itself is true.

What then I saw is more than tongue can say.
Our human speech is dark before the vision.
The ravished memory swoons and falls away.

So dazzling was the splendor of that Ray,
that I must certainly have lost my senses
had I, but for an instant, turned away.

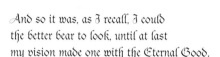

And so it was, as I recall, I could
the better bear to look, until at last
my vision made one with the Eternal Good.

Experiencing that Radiance, the spirit
is so indrawn it is impossible
even to think of ever turning from It.

Here my powers rest from their high fantasy,
but already I could feel my being turned ~
instinct and intellect balanced equally
as in a wheel whose motion nothing jars ~
by the Love that moves the Sun and the other stars.

NATIVITY OF

Today from the Aurora's bosom
A pink has fallen ~ a crimson blossom;
And oh, how glorious rests the hay
On which the fallen blossom lay!

When silence gently had unfurled
Her mantel over all below,
And crowned with winter's frost and snow,
Night swayed the sceptre of the world,
Amid the gloom descending slow
Upon the monarch's frozen bosom
A pink has fallen ~ a crimson blossom.

C·H·R·I·S·T

 Luis de Góngora

TRANSLATED FROM THE SPANISH BY HENRY WADSWORTH LONGFELLOW

The only flower the Virgin bore
(Aurora fair) within her breast,
She gave to earth, yet still possessed
Her virgin blossom as before;
That hay that colored drop caressed,
Received upon its faithful bosom
That single flower ∽ a crimson blossom.

The manger, unto which 'twas given,
Even amid wintry snows and cold,
Within its fostering arms to fold
The blushing flower that fell from heaven,
Was as a canopy of gold ∽
A downy couch, where on its bosom
That flower had fallen ∽ that crimson blossom.

O STAR

O Star of Galilee,
Shining over earth's dark sea,
Shed thy glorious light on me.

Queen of clemency and love,
Be my advocate above,
And through Christ all sin remove.

When the angel called thee blest,
And with transports filled thy breast,
Thy high Lord became thy guest.

Earth's purest creature thou,
In the heavens exulting now,
With a halo round thy brow.

OF GALILEE

 Girolamo Savonarola

TRANSLATED FROM THE LATIN BY R. R. MADDEN

Beauty beams in every trace
Of the Virgin Mother's face,
Full of glory and of grace ~

A Beacon to the just,
To the sinner hope and trust,
Joy of the angel host.

Ever glorified, thy throne
Is where thy blessed Son
Doth reign: Through Him alone ~

All pestilence shall cease,
And sin and strife decrease,
And the kingdom come of peace.

APPEAL FOR

And thou, O Virgin, Daughter, Mother, Bride
Of the same Lord, who gave to you each key
Of heaven and hell, and everything beside,
The day thy Gabriel said "All hail" to thee.

Since to thy servants pity's ne'er denied ~
With flowing rhymes, a pleasant style and free ~
Be to my verses, then, benignly kind,
And to the end illuminate my mind.

Illumination

Luigi Pulci

TRANSLATED FROM THE ITALIAN BY LORD BYRON

ODE TO THE

Fair Virgin,
Vestured with the sun!
Bright shining one,
Star crowned:
Who such sweet ultimate favor found
From all eternity
With the great primal Sun
That from the height
He stooped in thee to hide the light
Of His Divinity:
Now shall my love upraise
New measures in thy praise,
Though to begin without thy aid were vain

V I R G I N

Francesco Petrarch

TRANSLATED FROM THE ITALIAN BY HELEN LEE PEABODY

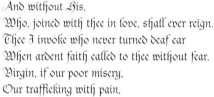

And without His,
Who, joined with thee in love, shall ever reign.
Thee I invoke who never turned deaf ear
When ardent faith called to thee without fear.
Virgin, if our poor misery,
Our trafficking with pain,
In thy deep heart stir pity,
Incline to me again.
Once more on thy sure succor now I lean,
Though of base clay am I
And thou be Heaven's queen.

O Virgin wise,
Of prudent virgins blest,
foremost and best

Beyond compare,
With shining lamp most clear,
Bright shield of the oppressed,
With thee we know
Not mere escape from evil fortune's blow
Or bitter death,
But triumph o'er the foe.
Thou who dost cool this flame
Which, blazing among mortals, love we name.
Virgin, turn thou thine eyes,
Sad eyes that watched beside
The piteous body of thy Son that died,
Unto my dubious state.
Thy counsel now I seek,
Disconsolate.

Pure Virgin, without stain,

God's daughter meet,

And by conception sweet

His mother too,

Thou, a keen brightness to our dark world sent,

Art high Heaven's ornament.

Through thee alone,

O lofty window gleaming with heavenly light,

Came God's Son and thine own,

To save us mortals from our desperate plight.

Among all dusty toilers of the earth,

Virgin most blessed,

Chosen wert thou, pure gold without alloy,

To turn Eve's sorrow into joy.

O make me of God's grace to worthy be,

Thou who art crowned in heaven eternally.
Virgin most holy, filled with every grace,
Who the sure path of true humility did trace
To the bright heavens where my prayers ascend,
Thou didst achieve the much desired end
That springs from fairest root.
Of Justice and of Piety art thou
The ripened fruit.
Three sweetest names unite
In thee alone,
Mother and spouse and daughter, all in one.
O Virgin glorious,
Sweet spouse of our high King
Who gloriously reigns,
Who freed us from our chains,

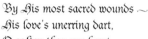

By His most sacred wounds ~
His love's unerring dart,
O soften thou my heart.

Virgin, in all this world unparalleled,
Heaven enamored is
Of thy pure bliss.
O thou, the living temple of high God,
Who thy virginity did fruitful make,
Most joyful for thy sake,
In spite of inner strife,
Is all my life.
Virgin most pious, sweet,
In whom all graces meet,
My spirit flows to thee,

Praying that thou wilt bend
The twisted fragments of my broken life
Unto a perfect end.

O Virgin, bathed in ever-living light,
Bright star of our tempestuous dark sea,
Thou faithful guide
To mariners that trust in thee.
Behold in what dread tempest I am tossed
Rudderless and alone,
Fearing myself for lost
With sinful soul I still in thee confide.
Virgin, I pray
Let not our common enemy deride
My bitter woe.

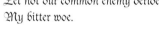
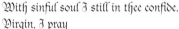

Remember that for man's sin
God took upon Himself our human flesh,
To thy sweet virgin cloister entering in.

Virgin, how many tears have I not shed,
What prayers have I not offered and in vain!
Sorrow and loss and fear of future pain,
All these have compassed me
Since my first breath I drew by Arno's side.
My searchings far and wide,
My acts, my words and mortal beauty
Have undone me quite.
Virgin, sacred of soul,
Do not delay,
for who can say

That I approach not to life's end.
And the long swiftly flowing years,
Swift as an arrow's dart,
Filled to the brim with bitter loss and tears,
Have left no other trace
Than a sure death which looks me in the face.
Virgin, she whom I mourn is now dry dust,
Who, living, caused me full a thousand woes,
But of my bitter throes
She knew not one,
Else had she honor lost, and I had been undone.
But thou, O heavenly Lady fair,
Our Goddess rare,
(If to speak thus of thee is meet)
Virgin of delicate high sentiment,
Thou sees all.

Others have failed to end my misery,
But now through thy great power can be wrought
Health to my soul, and honor unto thee.

Virgin, with whom my hope is most secure,
In need my refuge sure,
Let not thy gaze

Rest on unworthy me.
But rather see
Him who in likeness to Himself did raise

My fallen nature base,
Enduing it with grace,
Else might my eyes of error take their fill.

Medusa-like
My heart would turn to stone
And evil humors on the air distill.

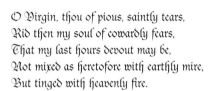

O Virgin, thou of pious, saintly tears,
Rid then my soul of cowardly fears,
That my last hours devout may be,
Not mixed as heretofore with earthly mire,
But tinged with heavenly fire.

Virgin, with human heart devoid of pride,
Humanity thou too didst take
By primal Love's decree.
With contrite heart I pray you pity me.
I that so faithful proved
To mortal lady, greatly, vainly loved,
So gentle art thou, shall I not love thee?
If from my sad and miserable state
By thy sweet hands I rise,

Virgin, I consecrate to thee
All my most treasured enterprise.
My dear imaginings,
My language and my thoughts, my pen, my heart,
My tears and sighs,
Be thou my guide to Heaven, nor fail to weigh
Celestial desires when I pray.
The day approaches now, so swift time flies,
Virgin, uniquely one,
Of my last end.
Pierced is my heart with thought of death;
Now to thy Son, true Man, true God, commend
My parting soul, that He may give release,
Receiving my last breath in peace.

CANTIGA

White and crimson, cheek and breast,
 O Virgin blest!

The pledge of love in Bethlehem
A flower was on the rose tree's stem,

O Virgin blest!

In Bethlehem in sign of love
The rose branch raised a rose above,

O Virgin blest!

In the rose came forth a flower ~
Jesus, our high Lord of Power,

O Virgin blest!

The Rose of all the rose tree's span,
God in nature and a Man ~

O Virgin blest!

Gil Vincente

TRANSLATED FROM THE SPANISH BY THOMAS WALSH

QUEEN OF THE

Queen of the Angels, Mary, thou whose smile
Adorns the heavens with their brightest ray;
Calm star that o'er the sea directs the way
Of wandering barks unto their homing isle.
By all the glory, Virgin without guile,
Relieve me of my grievous woes, I pray!
Protect me, save me from the snares that stay
Beyond to misdirect me and defile!

I trust in thee with that same trust of old,
Fixed in the ancient love and reverence
Which now I tell as I have always told.
Guide thou my journey, strenghten my pretense
To reach with thee at last the blessed fold
Thy Son prepares His flock in recompense.

A · N · G · E · L · S

 Giovanni Boccaccio

TRANSLATED FROM THE ITALIAN BY THOMAS WALSH

STABAT MATER

In shade of death's sad tree
Stood doleful she.
Ah she! Now by none other
Name to be known, alas, but sorrow's mother.
Before her eyes,
Hers, and the whole world's joys,
Hanging all torn she sees, and in His woes
And pains, her pangs and throes.
Each wound of His, from every part,
All, more at home in her own heart.

D O L O R O S A

 Jacopone da Todi

TRANSLATED FROM THE LATIN BY RICHARD CRASHAW

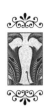

What kind of marble then
Is that cold man
Who can look on and see,
Nor keep such noble sorrows company?
Sure even from you
(My flints) some drops are due
To see so many unkind swords contest
So fast for one soft breast.
While with a faithful, mutual flood,
Her eyes bleed tears, his wounds weep blood.

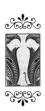

O costly intercourse
Of deaths and worse,
Divided loves. While son and mother
Discourse alternate wounds to one another;
Quick deaths that grow
And gather, as they come and go:
His nails write swords in her, which soon her heart
Pays back with more than their own smart.
Her swords, still growing with his pain,
Turn spears, and straight come home again.

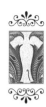

She sees her son, her God
Bow with the load
Of borrowed sins, and swim
In woes that were not made for Him.
Ah hard command
Of Love! Here must she stand
Charged to look on, and with a steadfast eye
She her life die:
Leaving her only so much breath
As serves to keep alive her death.

O Mother turtledove!
Soft source of love
That these dry lids might borrow
Something from thy full seas of sorrow!
O in that breast
Of thine (that noblest nest
Both of love's fires and floods) might I recline
This hard, cold heart of mine!
The chill lump would relent, and prove
Soft subject for the siege of love.

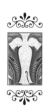

O teach those wounds to bleed
In me: Me, so to read
This book of loves, thus writ
In lines of death, my life may copy it
With loyal cares.
O let me, here, claim shares.
Yield something in thy sad prerogative
(Great Queen of griefs) and give
Me too my tears: Who, though all stone,
Think much that thou shouldst mourn alone.

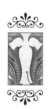

Yea let my life and me
Fix here with thee,
And at the humble foot
Of this fair tree take our eternal root.
That so we may
At least be in love's way.
And in these chaste wars while winged wounds flee
So fast twixt Him and thee,
My breast may catch the kiss of some kind dart,
Though as at second hand, from either heart.

O you, your own best darts
Dear, doleful hearts!
Hail and strike home and make me see
That wounded bosoms their own weapons be.
Come wounds! Come darts!
Nailed hands and pierced hearts!
Come your whole selves,
Sorrow's great son and mother!
Nor grudge a younger brother
Of griefs his portion, who (had all their due)
One single wound should not have left for you.

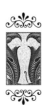

Shall I set there
So deep a share
(Dear wounds) and only now
In sorrows draw no dividend with you?
O be more wise
If not more soft, mine eyes!
Flow, tardy founts! Into descent showers
Dissolve my days and hours.
And if thou yet (faint soul!) defer
To bleed with Him, fail not to weep with Her.

Rich Queen, lend some relief,
At least an alms of grief
To a heart who by sad right of sin
Can prove the whole sum (too sure) due to Him.
By all those stings
Of love, sweet bitter things,
Which these torn hands transcribed on thy true heart
O teach mine too the art
To study Him so, till we mix
Wounds and become one crucifix.

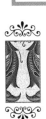

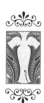

O let me suck the wine
So long of this chaste vine
Till drunk of the dear wounds, I be
A lost thing to the world, as it to me,
O faithful friend
Of me and of my end!
Fold up my life in love and lay it beneath
My dear Lord's vital death.
Lo, heart, thy hope's whole plea! Her precious breath
Poured out in prayers for thee; thy Lord's in death.

Renaissance Masterpieces

🍃 MADONNA AND CHILD by CARLO CRIVELLI, ca.1470 [DUST JACKET/FRONT; PAGE 59]. Tempera and gold leaf on wood, 14 ⅞ x 10 inches. Courtesy of The Metropolitan Museum of Art, New York. The Jules Bache Collection. Photograph © 1984 The Metropolitan Museum of Art 🍃 MADONNA THE MAGNIFICENT by SANDRO BOTTICELLI, ca.1483 [DUST JACKET/BACK; PAGE 55]. Tempera on wood, circular panel, 45 inches. Courtesy of Uffizi Gallery, Florence/Art Resource, New York. 🍃 LITTA MADONNA by LEONARDO DA VINCI, ca.1490 [PAGE 10]. Oil on panel, 16 ⅛ x 12 ⅞ inches. Courtesy of The State Hermitage Museum, St. Petersburg. 🍃 MADONNA OF THE TREES by GIOVANNI BELLINI, ca.1487 [PAGE 14]. Oil and tempera on panel, 29 x 22 ¾ inches. Courtesy of Galleria Dell'Accademia, Venice/Art Resource, New York. 🍃 VIRGIN ADORING THE CHILD by FRA FILIPPO LIPPI, ca.1459 [PAGE 22]. Oil on wood, 50 ½ x 46 ¼ inches. Courtesy of Bildarchiv Preussischer Kulturbesitz, Berlin. Photograph by Jörg P. Anders © 1999 Bildarchiv Preussischer Kulturbesitz. 🍃 VIRGIN AND CHILD by JOOS VAN CLEVE AND WORKSHOP, ca.1525 [PAGE 28]. Tempera and oil on wood, 28 ⅛ x 21¼ inches. Courtesy of The Metropolitan Museum of Art, New York. The Jack and Belle Linsky Collection. Photograph © 1983 The Metropolitan Museum of Art. 🍃 VIRGIN AND CHILD UNDER THE APPLE TREE by LUCAS CRANACH THE ELDER, ca.1523 [PAGE 35]. Oil on canvas, 34 x 23 inches. Courtesy of The State Hermitage Museum, St. Petersburg. 🍃 MADONNA WITH THE RED APPLE [aka *The Virgin and Martin van Nieuwenhove*] by HANS MEMLING, ca.1487 [PAGE 42]. Oil and tempera on wood, 17 ¼ x 13 inches, diptych. Courtesy of Memlingmuseum, Sint-Janshospitaal Stedelijke Musea, Bruges. 🍃 VIRGIN AND CHILD by JEAN FOUQUET, ca.1443 [PAGE 44]. Oil and tempera on panel, 32 x 37 inches. Courtesy of Koninklijk Museum voor Schone Kunsten, Antwerp. 🍃 MADONNA OF BURGOMASTER MEYER by HANS HOLBEIN THE YOUNGER, ca.1526 [PAGE 46]. Oil on wood, 58 x 41 inches. Courtesy of Hessische Hausstiftung, Schlossmuseum, Darmstadt.

PUBLISHED IN 1999 BY STEWART, TABORI & CHANG.
A DIVISION OF U.S. MEDIA HOLDINGS, INC.
115 WEST 18 STREET,
NEW YORK, NY 10011

DISTRIBUTED IN CANADA BY GENERAL PUBLISHING COMPANY LTD,
30 LESMILL ROAD, DON MILLS, ONTARIO, CANADA M3B 2T6

🐚 IN GLORY · BLESSED VIRGIN MARY EDITORIAL DIRECTOR: ZILLAH BAHAR 🐚

LIBRARY OF CONGRESS CATALOGING-IN-PUBLICATION DATA
IN GLORY, BLESSED VIRGIN MARY : POEMS & PRAYERS
P. CN.
ISBN: 1-55670-935-8
1. MARY, BLESSED VIRGIN, SAINT POETRY. 2. MARY, BLESSED VIRGIN,
SAINT — ART. 3. PRAYERS.
PN6110.M28149 1999
232.91 — DC21   99-28665
CIP

PRINTED IN SINGAPORE

10 9 8 7 6 5 4 3 2 1

FIRST PRINTING

PRODUCTIONS

IN GLORY · BLESSED VIRGIN MARY IS THE CREATION OF

FLY PRODUCTIONS, SAN FRANCISCO

~

~

UNCOMMON THANKS TO

OUR OUTSTANDING PUBLISHER

AND BRILLIANT EDITOR AT

STEWART, TABORI & CHANG

🐝

LESLIE STOKER AND HELENE DeRADE CAMPBELL